HISTORY BENEATH YOUR FEET

ANCIENT ROME

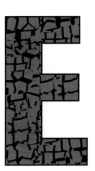

SEAN SHEEHAN

RSVP

RAINTREE
STECK-VAUGHN
PUBLISHERS
A Steck-Vaughn Company

Austin, Texas
www.steck-vaughn.com

History Beneath Your Feet

Titles in this series

Ancient Egypt
Ancient Greece
Ancient Rome
The Aztecs

© Copyright 2000, text, Steck-Vaughn Company

Published by Raintree Steck-Vaughn Publishers, an imprint of Steck-Vaughn Company

Library of Congress Cataloging-in-Publication Data
Sheehan, Sean.
Ancient Rome / Sean Sheehan.
     p.   cm.—(History beneath your feet)
     Includes bibliographical references and index.
     Summary: Highlights the many archaeological digs and findings in Rome and discusses what life was like in ancient Rome.
     ISBN 0-8172-5752-7
     1. Rome—Civilization—Juvenile literature.
     2. Archaeology—Juvenile literature.
     [1. Rome—Civilization. 2. Archaeology.]
     I. Title. II. Title: Rome. III. Series.
     DG77.S46   1999
     937—dc21   99-26532

Printed in Italy. Bound in the United States.
1 2 3 4 5 6 7 8 9 0 04 03 02 01 00

Cover photographs: The Colosseum, Roman brooch (Wayland Picture Library)

The publishers would like to thank the following for permission to publish their pictures (t=top; b=bottom)

Lesley and Roy Adkins 6, 8, 11, 20b, 28, 36, 38, 40, 41, 42, 43; AKG London 4–5, 13, 16, 18, 19b, 30, 32, 33, 39; C. M. Dixon 9, 10, 17, 20t, 34t; Peter Hicks 7, 29b, 34b, 35; Michael Holford 37; Norma Joseph 15, 25t; Planet Earth Pictures 12; Popperfoto 14; Wayland Picture Library 19t, 21, 22t, 22b, 23, 24, 26t, 26b, 27t, 27b, 29t; Werner Forman Archive 25b

CONTENTS

WHAT IS ARCHAEOLOGY?

"Archaeology" is a Greek word meaning "the study of ancient things." Archaeologists study the remains of people, buildings, and objects from earlier times and then piece together what life was like in the distant past. Some of these remains are so old that they have become hidden by earth or more recent buildings. This means that archaeologists first have to find where these remains are hidden, and then dig down or "excavate" to see what is there. This is why so much history is "beneath your feet."

WHO WERE THE ANCIENT ROMANS?

Rome is the capital of Italy, and its archaeology goes back to the tenth century B.C. Archaeologists have found evidence from around this time of small hilltop villages near the mouth of the Tiber River. By the sixth century B.C., Rome was an important town that had developed from these villages.

The first rulers of early Rome were kings. Several of these kings came from Etruria, an older civilization to the north of Italy. Romans were not influenced by Etruria alone. They also learned from the culture of Greece, first from Greek colonists who had settled in southern Italy and Sicily, and later from Greece itself after it became part of the Roman world.

The Romans were ruled by kings until the sixth century B.C. A republic was then established, which lasted until 27 B.C. when Augustus became the first of a long line of emperors.

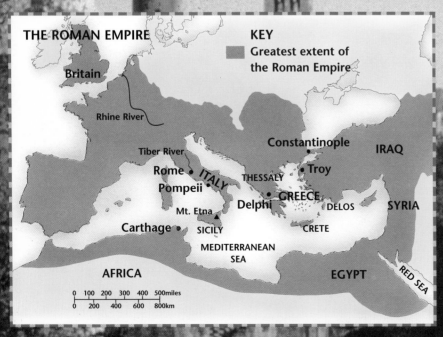

THE ROMAN EMPIRE

KEY
Greatest extent of the Roman Empire

Britain
Rhine River
Constantinople
IRAQ
Tiber River
Rome • ITALY
THESSALY
• Troy
Pompeii
• GREECE
Delphi
DELOS
SYRIA
Mt. Etna
CRETE
Carthage
SICILY
MEDITERRANEAN
SEA
AFRICA
EGYPT
RED SEA

0 100 200 300 400 500miles
0   200   400   600   800km

As the Empire expanded, Romans settled in colonies outside Rome, and by A.D. 48 there were about six million Roman citizens spread around the Mediterranean area. In Rome itself, with a population of over one million, there were probably two slaves for every free citizen. Slavery was essential to the Romans, and so was their army. Without the might of the legions, the Roman world would not have extended so far or so quickly.

The Empire became so large that by the end of the third century A.D. it had been split into an eastern and a western half. The western Empire came to an end in the fifth century A.D., but the eastern Empire, with its capital, Constantinople, continued to exist until 1453. Not counting this eastern empire, Roman civilization lasted for over a thousand years. At the height of its power, the Empire stretched from Britain in the West to Syria in the East and included the whole of the Mediterranean area.

The Forum was Rome's city center. The three columns on the right are the remains of a temple that once stood there.

LOOKING FOR CLUES

Archaeologists are like detectives who search for clues. Just as detectives search the scene of a crime, archaeologists excavate sites where they hope to uncover evidence of how people lived in the past.

When archaeology first became popular, it was more like a treasure hunt than an investigation. Europeans were eager to find important sites where they hoped to unearth valuable objects. What they found was often packed up and shipped home to their own country, where it could be sold or displayed in a museum. Archaeologists today have a different attitude and are far more careful about what they do.

Ancient buildings quickly become overgrown and will eventually be obscured from sight. Archaeologists must first clear a site before structures like this temple can be properly examined.

This aerial photograph of a Roman fort, at Hardknott in the north of England, shows the fort walls enclosing (left to right) granaries, the headquarters, and the house of the commanding officer.

Many Roman buildings and monuments are still standing, but archaeologists often have to dig beneath the ground to find evidence of the past. That is because buildings fall down and become buried over time. Vegetation may grow over a site, or new buildings may be constructed on top of the ruins of older ones. Archaeologists frequently have to dig down 10 feet (3 m) or more before any useful finds are revealed.

In order to locate possible sites, archaeologists use aerial photography, which can reveal important clues. In France, for example, evidence of hundreds of Roman country houses and farm buildings has been identified from the air.

AERIAL ARCHAEOLOGY

In the countryside in dry weather, a road or a stone floor buried under the ground may cause plants to wither because water cannot get through. This is known as a crop mark and can be seen from the air. A filled-in pit on the other hand, which might turn out to be a Roman garbage dump, produces rich soil that may also affect the appearance of crops and will also be visible from the air.

Pale-colored stones were often used for Roman buildings, and a farmer plowing fields may accidentally reveal the outline of settlements that will show up clearly in an aerial photograph. A lot of what is known about the location of Roman frontier forts in desert areas in the Middle East and North Africa has been gained from aerial photography.

PIECING TOGETHER THE EVIDENCE

The excavation of a site is a very well-organized affair, because archaeologists want to make sure that they do not overlook any important evidence. When excavating a Roman country villa, for example, different teams will work on different sections, carefully recording and cleaning what they find. At the end of a dig, they will probably have revealed the remains of walls, indicating different rooms, and many artifacts, such as statues, pottery shards, tools, and even human bones. Archaeologists then have to piece together these different clues to build a picture of life in the villa.

These archaeologists are carefully cleaning the excavated remains of a Roman villa on the actual site.

For example, the excavation of a large villa north of Rome revealed a lot about Roman food and drink. Grape juice was prepared in a special room before being drained into a cellar where it was fermented to make wine. This tells us how important wine was to the Romans. Another room was used for processing olives. As well as being a source of food, olive oil was used for cooking and for fueling oil lamps.

BOTANICAL ARCHAEOLOGY

When the town of Pompeii was buried by the volcanic ash from Vesuvius, the plants all died, but evidence of them remained. As the roots of plants decayed, they left spaces that either remained hollow or filled with ash. By carefully clearing the spaces and filling them with cement, an American archaeologist, Wilhelmina Jashemsky, made casts of the roots and was able to identify the plants. In one vineyard grapevines had been carefully planted 13 ft. (4 m) apart, each one supported by a wooden stake. Over 50 trees had also been planted. Some of these have been recognized as olive trees from their roots. Pompeii was a green city not just because the houses had ornamental gardens but also because a lot of food was grown inside the town.

Most excavations of Roman sites reveal only a small fragment of what was there originally. However, the eruption of the volcano Mount Vesuvius in A.D. 79 resulted in the preservation of a whole town. Pompeii, a town built on the slopes of the mountain, was buried beneath a layer of volcanic ash, which protected it from the elements and the ravages of time. Excavating Pompeii has provided a tremendous amount of information about Roman life. Whole buildings and streets have been discovered. As the terrified inhabitants ran for their lives, everything was left exactly as it was. Archaeologists have even found a table set for lunch, showing that ordinary people ate bread and eggs with salad and fruit.

This excavated wine press from Pompeii shows how a wooden wheel was used to turn a timber pole so that grapes could be crushed on a large scale.

TRANSPORTATION AND TRADE

The expansion of the Roman Empire depended on its transportation system. Road builders and engineers traveled with the Roman Army, and roads were laid down quickly so that supplies and reinforcements could be transported easily. The roads were also important because they allowed messengers carrying news or orders to travel quickly.

The Roman road network covered the whole Empire: some 53,000 mi. (85,000 km) of roads in all. Archaeologists have examined the remains of Roman roads, many of which still survive in good condition, and have been able to see how they were built. The method of construction varied according to the type of land on which the road was being built.

The first real roads in Europe were built by the Romans, and their engineers knew that a layer of rubble would provide a firm foundation for a road surface.

ALL ROADS LEAD TO ROME

Because Rome was the center of the Empire for hundreds of years, a number of important roads led from it to different parts of Europe. This is the origin of the famous expression "all roads lead to Rome." The first great road to be built out of Rome was the Appian Way, which linked the capital with the port of Brindisi. The Romans had so many roads at the height of the Empire that road maps were drawn to help people plan long journeys, showing the distances between settlements on a highway.

Roman roads were built to last. The Appian Way, built in 312 B.C., can still be walked along today.

Roman engineers knew that a road would last only if the foundations were carefully laid and kept as dry as possible. If the ground was soft, a frame of logs or layers of sand was used as a foundation on which to spread a layer of clay. Flat or crushed stones were then cemented into the clay and a surface of smaller cobbled stones or gravel was laid on top. If the ground was hard, the foundation was made from layers of large stones and gravel. The top surface was laid down in a slight arch, known as a camber, so that rainwater would drain off to either side. Important roads had curbstones laid at the sides and had a narrow ditch on either side that drained away water during heavy rainfall.

MERCHANT SHIPPING

The Mediterranean Sea was also essential to the Romans, and they sailed across it in all directions. Much of what is known about Roman ships and transportation by sea comes from underwater archaeology. The remains of sunken ships settle on the floor of the sea, and the surrounding silt acts as a preservative. Because of this, hundreds of Roman wrecks have been located, some with well-preserved cargoes. In this sense the Mediterranean is the largest ancient Roman museum in the world.

An underwater archaeologist checks the condition of a Roman amphora that has lain undamaged at the bottom of the sea for centuries.

UNDERWATER ARCHAEOLOGY

Archaeologists can spend only about three hours a day working underwater. Otherwise, they risk the danger of decompression sickness, known as the bends. If the wreck is more than 100 ft. (30 m) below the surface, the diver can make only two 20-minute dives a day, with a break of a few hours between each dive. A video camera and a strong measuring tape are used to map the wreck. Scaffolding may be erected close to the wreck so that detailed measurements and photographs can be taken more accurately. Special equipment like an airlift (a sort of underwater vacuum cleaner) may be needed in order to remove the sediment that has helped preserve the wreck.

Harbors were built for larger ships, using a form of concrete that would set underwater. Excavations near the Thames River in London have revealed waterfronts made of timbers, and evidence of Roman riverboats has been discovered in the silt of the Rhine River in Germany. Riverboats were designed like large hollowed logs with flat bottoms, which allowed them to travel along shallow inland rivers.

Roman merchant ships carried most of their cargo in storage pots known as amphorae. Shaped like a carrot or a bulb, an amphora had a pair of handles at the top and a pointed or flat bottom. They could be stacked in layers on a ship with the pointed ends of one layer fitting between the necks of those underneath. Archaeologists were able to calculate that a Roman ship sunk in the first century B.C. could carry about 7,000 amphorae, each weighing 110 lbs. (50 kg). It would be another 1,500 years before ships of this size were built again in Europe.

Scientific tests help archaeologists learn what was stored in amphorae. Traces of olive oil, grain, and wine have all been found, as well as a famous ancient Roman fish sauce called *garum*. This was a popular ingredient in cooking and was transported by ship all over the Roman world.

This wall painting shows two piers at the entrance to a Roman port and a number of ships safely anchored.

IMAGES OF THE PAST

Historians use written records to find out about the past, but the Romans did not write in detail about every part of their lives. Nor can archaeologists find the physical remains of everything they would like to know about. That is why pictures of Roman life are so important to archaeologists and historians. The most common pictures are mosaics, wall paintings, and reliefs.

MOSAICS

Roman houses had no carpets or wallpaper, but people who could afford it decorated their homes with pictures. At first, patterned floors were made using small black-and-white cubes of stone. Then came a fashion for more colorful and adventurous designs. Colored stones, glass, and tiles were cut into tiny pieces and used to make mosaic pictures.

At the buried town of Pompeii, archaeologists have discovered and carefully cleaned a number of mosaic floors. One of them shows a group of actors dressing up in their costumes for a play. Only men could act in plays; we see a man dressed as a woman and playing music while two actors appear to be practicing their dance steps. The musical instrument is a double flute. We also see various stage masks that the actors used in their performances.

Craftsmen who laid floors such as this were highly regarded in ancient Rome. This floor, discovered in Israel, is in extremely good condition and is being carefully restored by an archaeologist.

PROJECT: DESIGN A MOSAIC

You will need:
A large sheet of plain cardboard
Colored or painted cardboard
Glue or paste
Scissors

Begin by drawing your design onto the large sheet of cardboard. Use the mosaic designs shown in this chapter for ideas. Cut up the colored cardboard into small squares. The more detailed you want your mosaic to be, the smaller the squares will have to be. Glue the small squares to your design.

Another mosaic floor shows various fish. The pictures are realistic enough for the types of fish to be identified, telling us the kinds of fish the ancient Romans liked to eat.

Actors' masks served as a kind of microphone to help project the voice, and the expression on the mask indicated the kind of role the actor was playing.

WALL PAINTINGS AND RELIEFS

Walls were smoothly plastered and then painted with pictures. Portraits were popular, and from these we are able to see what Roman people looked like. We can see their hairstyles, the clothes and jewelry they wore, and the expressions on their faces.

As well as mosaics and wall paintings, archaeologists have unearthed pictures carved out of stone, marble, and clay. These are known as reliefs, and they are often found decorating a tomb. Even former slaves who had become Roman citizens had tombs. Their portraits were carved from a block and set into one side of the tomb. If they were carpenters, for example, pictures of their woodworking tools would also appear on their tombs.

Paintings, mosaics, and reliefs can bring alive Roman life. They remind us that in many ways ordinary Romans were people who went about their lives much as we do. A stone relief shows a woman waiting in a butcher's shop. She appears to be holding a shopping list in her hand. One small part of a mosaic shows a woman dancing with castanets.

A Roman woman and her husband, thought to be a lawyer. Wall paintings like this reveal a great deal about the way people dressed, how they wore their hair, and sometimes, as in this case, their occupations in life.

IDEAS FROM ABROAD

The Roman Empire covered such a large area that it was always possible to learn new ideas and techniques from foreign countries. The art of floor mosaics was learned from northern Greece. The Romans were also attracted by the myths and legends of ancient Greece. Some of the wall paintings found in the houses at Pompeii and nearby Herculaneum tell the stories of Greek heroes such as Hercules.

Other areas of Roman life were very different from ours. A mosaic from Sicily shows a wounded man on the ground while his companions try to protect him from a wild boar. They had been hunting the animal for food. When people were injured there were no pain-killing injections or pills. This is made clear by a wall painting that shows a man standing up awake while a doctor operates on his thigh.

This scene is taken from the tomb of a butcher and shows joints of meat and weighing scales hanging from hooks on the wall of his shop. The butcher himself is preparing a cut of meat for a customer, who has her shopping list in her hand.

A DAY AT THE GAMES

Pictures found by archaeologists tell us that many Romans enjoyed watching acts of cruelty. Slaves and prisoners who were trained to fight each other for public entertainment were called gladiators. A mosaic shows one of the most common type of fighters. He is carrying his net and holding a three-pronged spear called a trident. He was called a *retiarius*, a net man, and his opponent would have some body protection as well as a sword. We know that women also used to fight in a public show. A stone relief, which is now in London's British Museum, shows two female gladiators fighting with daggers. They are not wearing helmets and have only shields to protect them.

A mosaic showing two gladiators being put through their paces by their trainer, who was called a lanista. Lanistae, who were often ex-gladiators themselves, were employed by the wealthy owners of the gladiatorial schools to make sure that their gladiators had the best chance of victory in the arena.

DEATH IN THE ARENA

The death of wild animals, criminals, and gladiators in the arena was a popular spectacle in ancient Rome for hundreds of years. In 65 B.C., Julius Caesar organized a public show in which over 300 pairs of gladiators fought to the death in a single day. The Emperor Nero had 400 bears and 300 lions killed on the same day of a show. When the famous amphitheater in Rome known as the Colosseum was first opened in A.D. 80 by the Emperor Titus, 5,000 animals were killed in the arena. Twenty years later the Emperor Trajan bettered this by having 11,000 animals killed during a show at the Colosseum. The ancient Romans' love of death in the arena led to lions' being wiped out in Mesopotamia (Iraq).

Like most Roman public buildings, the Colosseum was built using slave labor. Slaves were also used to build a special road that was used to bring the blocks of stone for the Colosseum from quarries outside Rome.

A mosaic shows an antelope being pulled onto a ship, showing us that wild animals were collected in foreign places like North Africa and taken to Rome. This was very common because many thousands of animals were killed in public shows. A day's entertainment would begin in the morning with the killing of lions, leopards, tigers, elephants, bears, and other animals. They might be forced to fight each other or be killed by hunters.

These shows were free, and they attracted huge crowds. One wall painting shows that large canvas sunshades were erected at these shows to keep the heat of the sun off the audience. The same painting shows a fight breaking out between different crowds of supporters.

This magnificent carving shows a Roman lion hunt. Lions were captured alive so that they could be killed in the arena.

ARTIFACTS AND EVERYDAY LIFE

What artifacts of our everyday life might be found by archaeologists in the future? It is likely that some would be made of plastic, a material that is used for many purposes and does not easily perish. Bone has been called the "plastic" of the Romans. It could be finely carved into a variety of shapes and even cut open and filled. Many household items were made of this material, including hairpins, needles, combs, handles for knives and swords, and dice.

Dice have been found that are deliberately weighted on one side so that a player could cheat while playing a game.

This iron knife has a bone handle, which made it comfortable and easy to use.

Sometimes archaeologists are lucky, and they discover artifacts in an environment that preserves what would normally perish. A waterlogged site, for example, may preserve wooden or leather artifacts. At Vindolanda, a Roman fort in the north of England, such a site has revealed axles and tent pegs used by the Roman soldiers. Such artifacts tell us about the standard of work that went into such ordinary objects. The water also helped preserve a child's sock that had been sewn together from a piece of fabric.

The leather sole of a Roman shoe, preserved for centuries in a waterlogged site, being carefully cleaned by an archaeologist

The rarest find at Vindolanda was a collection of writing tablets with examples of Roman handwriting. The content of the writing—dealing with deliveries of food to the fort as well as fragments of personal letters—is less important to many historians and archaeologists than the actual examples of the everyday language of the Romans. Just as with English, the language of everyday Latin in the Roman world was not the same as that found on inscriptions or in works of literature.

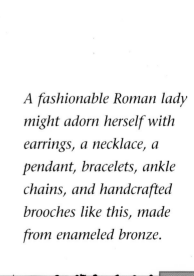

A fashionable Roman lady might adorn herself with earrings, a necklace, a pendant, bracelets, ankle chains, and handcrafted brooches like this, made from enameled bronze.

Like paintings and mosaics, the discovery of artifacts shows us that many aspects of Roman life were not very different from our own. Leather sandals, the bottom half of a bikini-style leather garment, pens and inkwells, jewelry, thimbles, locks and keys, whistles, toilet chains, dogtags, flutes, and cymbals have all been found. A fragment of one letter from Vindolanda is a friend's invitation to a birthday party. Such artifacts help us bring to life a familiar world where ordinary Romans went about their daily lives in a way that we can understand.

Other artifacts remind us that not everyone in the Roman world had the same rights. Although some slaves were well treated, others had very hard lives and were bought and sold like cattle. Manacles have been found that chained the slaves by their feet to prevent their escape.

Signet rings such as this, when pressed onto wax, served as a form of identification. Each ring was therefore individually designed for its owner.

Brooches were essential for holding cloaks, gowns, and tunics together.

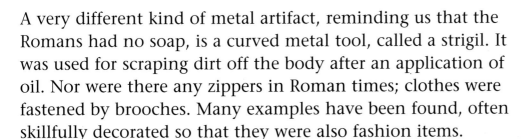

A very different kind of metal artifact, reminding us that the Romans had no soap, is a curved metal tool, called a strigil. It was used for scraping dirt off the body after an application of oil. Nor were there any zippers in Roman times; clothes were fastened by brooches. Many examples have been found, often skillfully decorated so that they were also fashion items.

A well-preserved example of two strigils, complete with their own jar for storing body oil

PRESERVING ARTIFACTS

Different types of artifacts require different preservation techniques. Fabrics and wooden artifacts, perhaps over 2,000 years old, cannot simply be taken away and placed in a museum. It takes time for specialists to prepare an artifact for public show; they will consider air pollution, temperature, and lighting. If in the first place a lack of oxygen preserved the artifact from natural decay, then exposure to air and bacteria will eventually destroy it. Other artifacts may require special cleaning, and especially with pottery, some parts may be repaired or even replaced. Museums often have special equipment that monitors temperature and humidity to make sure artifacts are kept in the right kind of environment.

MONEY TALKS

Although ancient Roman coins do not carry dates, dates can be very accurately determined from the portrait of the ruler and the writing. Archaeologists are also interested in where they find the coins. Many skeletons at Pompeii were found with purses of small coins. This tells archaeologists that ordinary people used money on a daily basis in much the same way we do. Larger collections of gold and silver coins were found alongside skeletons of people who were trying to escape the disaster. We can tell from this that some people were trying to protect the money they had saved.

Unlike our coins today, Roman coins contained real silver and gold. Archaeologists have made scientific studies of Roman coins to find out how much valuable metal they contained. For well over 100 years after Augustus became the first emperor in 27 B.C., the amount of silver in the denarius remained very high most of the time. After A.D. 150, however, the Romans put less silver in their coins, and in the third century A.D. the denarius became mostly bronze with a tiny amount of silver. This fits in with what we know about the difficult times in the third century A.D., with emperors struggling for power and attacks

A portrait of Brutus and a cap of liberty with daggers, celebrating the murder of Julius Caesar on the Ides (the 15th) of March, 44 B.C.

coming from enemies outside the Empire. Older, purer, coins were melted down, and their silver was used to make more money to pay for armies and other expenses.

Part of a wall painting from Pompeii, showing piles of silver and bronze coins on a writing desk

THE FACE OF MONEY

During the Roman Republic three officials were responsible for the production of the bronze, silver, and gold coins. Their names would appear on one side of the coin. (Something similar is still the case with British and American banknotes.) In Imperial Rome the face of the ruling emperor frequently appeared on coins, although sometimes they featured the face of the emperor's wife, daughter, or niece. When Nero became emperor in A.D. 54 his face appeared alongside that of his mother, probably because she had helped him become emperor. Important events, like the conquest of Britain under the Emperor Claudius in A.D. 43 or the conquest of Judea by the Emperor Vespasian in A.D. 70, were celebrated by a special-issue coin. Julius Caesar was the first Roman to be shown on a coin during his own lifetime.

Nero was only 16 when he became emperor, and his only rival for the throne was probably poisoned by Nero's mother, Agrippina, shown facing him on this coin.

POTS OF INFORMATION

Archaeologists commonly find more pottery than any other type of artifact. Since it is made of hard-baked clay, pottery can resist rotting and corrosion far better than most wooden or metal artifacts. Another reason that archaeologists so often find pottery is that it was extremely common throughout the Roman world. Millions of people cooked their meals, set their tables, and stored their food using items made of Roman pottery.

Rich people could afford fine pottery tableware covered with a smooth finish, known as a glaze. Colorful decorations painted or crafted by hand were added. Poorer families used plain, unglazed tableware, though many people could afford pottery with a thin glaze that gave a glossy appearance.

Look under your plates at home and you should find some writing telling you who made them or where they were produced. Roman pottery was no different, and by studying the names, archaeologists can build up a picture of the Roman pottery industry.

This popular type of pottery beaker dates from toward the end of the Empire.

This type of cup was often molded by hand and finished on a potter's wheel, with the decoration being added later when the clay was dry but still pliable.

THERMOLUMINESCENCE

There is a special technique for the dating of pottery called thermoluminescence. It is based on the fact that clay absorbs tiny amounts of radioactivity that, when heated ("thermo" means hot), release tiny amounts of light. By heating the pottery and measuring the released light, it is possible to have a rough idea of the pot's age. This method has been used to reveal forgeries. On a Roman site in Britain, thermoluminescence tests proved that tiles thought to be Roman were in fact fakes from the nineteenth century.

Some workshops employed as many as 60 skilled potters, each with a personal name stamp. A second signature would appear on the pottery if a specialist worked on an individual finish or a mold-maker added decorative details.

As the Empire expanded more and more, people wanted to enjoy the Roman lifestyle. A favorite kind of pottery, called "Samian ware," was orange-red and made in Gaul (modern France). The distinctive color was achieved by allowing a rich supply of oxygen into the kiln. This popular pottery was transported to most parts of the Empire.

"Samian ware," showing the distinctive red color produced by letting plenty of air into the kiln. Cutting off the air supply toward the end of baking produced a gray or black color.

After the collapse of the Empire it would take more than a thousand years before ordinary people in Europe could once again afford the kind of pottery that was commonplace in the Roman world.

The fine decoration on this vase, found in Great Britain, would have increased its price for the buyer.

WORKING WITH THE DEAD

When archaeologists excavate an ancient Roman site, they may come across skeletons. Careful study of these skeletons provides useful information about the people who lived, worked, and died in the Roman world. We know, for example, that the average height of a person living in Roman Britain was about 5 ft. 3 in. (1.6 m).

Archaeologists excavating a Roman skeleton. Great care is needed to avoid damage to the bones.

The age of a skeleton can be told from the bones and teeth; this information tells us that the average Roman citizen had a far shorter life than ours. It is thought that less than 50 percent of the people lived to be older than 50.

Sometimes the skeleton provides a clue to the cause of death. Diseases of the bone may be caused by a lack of vitamin D, and this lack has been discovered in some Roman skeletons. Vitamin D comes from fresh food and sunshine, and in northern Europe in the winter months both of these were lacking.

Archaeologists have also found urns containing human ashes, and the remains of coffins. This tells us that both cremation and burial were practiced by the Romans. Some coffins were made of lead, and attempts were sometimes made to preserve the body. Only well-off people could afford this kind of funeral. Most people were buried in wooden coffins or simply in a shroud, which have long since decayed under the ground.

Animal bones are often found when Roman temples are excavated—evidence of the Roman practice of sacrificing animals to the gods. Sometimes, however, the skeletons of animals have been found because a favorite pet has been buried. In Somerset, England, the skeletons of a man and his dog who had been buried together were excavated.

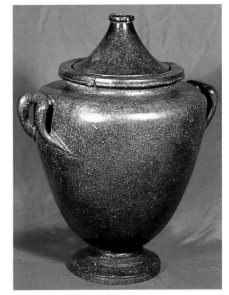

Only well-off Romans could afford a cremation, and urns like this were made to receive their ashes. Sometimes an inscription giving details about the dead person is found on the side of an urn.

PRESERVED IN PLASTER

An Italian archaeologist, Giuseppe Fiorelli, developed an interesting method of discovering the size and shape of people buried in ashes at Pompeii. The volcanic ash formed a hard shell around the body of the unlucky victim; although the body decayed, the person's shape was preserved as a hollow space. Plaster was poured into the space, which was empty except for the skeleton. Then the crust of ash was removed to reveal the exact shape and position of the body. This method also preserves impressions of sandals and clothing worn by the victim. Sometimes even the expression on the face of an unlucky person has been preserved by the plaster cast.

Fiorelli, who invented his plaster-casting technique in 1863, established archaeological work at Pompeii on a scientific basis, directing the work of 500 workmen and keeping records of all that was done.

BUILDINGS

The Romans were great builders and engineers. Archaeologists are lucky enough to have complete, or near-complete, buildings to examine. They include a number of houses and other buildings from the towns of Pompeii and Herculaneum, as well as the famous Colosseum in Rome where the gladiators fought.

An important reason why so many large buildings still stand is the Roman invention of concrete. They discovered that a certain volcanic earth could be mixed with lime to make a waterproof cement. They then learned to make concrete by adding bits of rock and broken bricks to the cement.

The Romans knew how important it was to have a reliable supply of water, and they constructed huge aqueducts to carry fresh water to their towns and cities. The fact that large-scale buildings like these have survived proves how skillful the Roman engineers were.

The Pont du Gard aqueduct near Nîmes, France. Ancient Rome had eleven aqueducts, one carrying water over a distance of 43 mi. (70 km).

PROJECT: AN ARCH EXPERIMENT

The arch was an important architectural technique because it spread the weight of a structure between the stones of the arch and downward onto the supporting wall or columns. In this experiment you will use the same building principles as the Romans to construct a model arch.

You will need:
Cardboard tube from a roll of paper towel
Modeling clay
Two large matchboxes (or building blocks of similar size)
Glue

1. Cut the cardboard tube in half and glue one half in a sideways position on top of the other half. This will be the "scaffold" for the arch.
2. Use the matchboxes to make two "columns" on either side of the scaffold, as shown.
3. Make five blocks for the arch from modeling clay. Each block should narrow a little at one end, as shown.
4. Starting at the ends, lay an equal number of clay blocks side by side around the curved half of the cardboard tube. Place the last block in the middle so that it locks the others together. Now remove the "scaffold" and see if your arch is able to support its own weight.

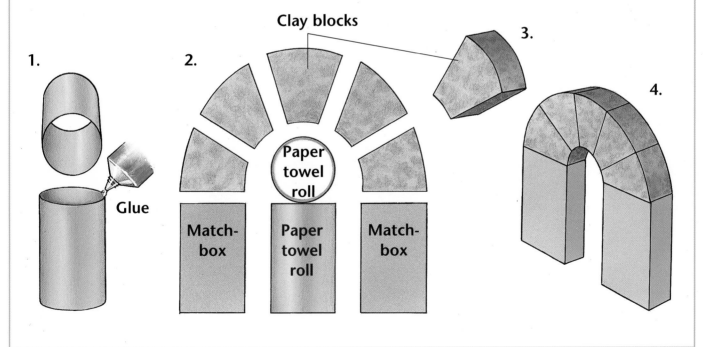

The building of arches was known before the Romans but never on the grand scale of the Pont du Gard aqueduct in France. Here, water had to be carried across a deep gorge, and Roman engineers designed and built an aqueduct with three stories of arches. It still stands, some 164 ft. (50 m) above the river.

The skill of Roman architects and builders, along with the invention of concrete, allowed them to construct impressive public buildings all over the empire. For example, the Pantheon in Rome has the largest dome ever built in the ancient world. The dome measures over 130 ft. (40 m) in diameter and has one circular hole in the center, 26 ft. (8 m) wide, which lets in enough light to illuminate the whole building even when the doors are closed. The Pantheon was built between A.D. 118 and 125 as a "temple to all the gods," and can still be visited today.

The Pantheon could not have been built without concrete, invented when Romans discovered a brown-colored volcanic earth that could form a cement that could then be strengthened with stones and broken bricks.

The scale of Roman theaters is equally impressive. The largest of modern theaters can hold only two to three thousand people at most. Roman theaters held up to eight times as many spectators: the theater at Ephesus, in modern Turkey, could seat up to 24,000 people! Even more astonishing was the Circus Maximus in Rome, where a quarter of a million people could watch the chariot races.

The Roman theater at Ephesus. Although deserted for the purpose of this photograph, the theater is an extremely popular tourist attraction.

CIRCUSES

Special stadiums, known as circuses, were built for chariot races. The basic design was always that of a long rectangle with one end rounded off like a semicircle. The huge Circus Maximus in Rome was 2,000 ft. (600 m) long, and chariots raced around in seven laps to complete one race. The dropping of a white cloth and the blowing of a trumpet was the signal for a race to begin. The most exciting and dangerous part of the contest was when the chariots raced at high speed around the semicircular bend. Charioteers could easily be killed, but the winners who survived became superstars of the ancient sports world.

HOUSES AND BATHS

Roman houses have been excavated in many parts of the Roman world. Rooms were built around a central courtyard, the *atrium*. At the back of the house there might be a garden court, the *peristyle*, with a fountain.

Not everyone could afford to live in a single-story house like this. In small towns many people lived in apartments that were above stores. They usually had separate outdoor staircases. In big cities like Rome, there were buildings, some of which were six or seven stories high, with small apartments (*insulae*).

The vast majority of ordinary Romans lived in apartments, where life was not as comfortable as this model might suggest.

A peristyle garden in Pompeii

Most apartments did not have their own toilets or washrooms, but public toilets and bathhouses have both been excavated. The foundations of bathhouses show clearly how the floor rested upon small pillars of tiles or bricks. This was known as a hypocaust. A fire, maintained by slaves, sent hot air under the building where it circulated in the spaces between the pillars.

An excavated Roman bathhouse showing the remains of the hypocaust heating system. Every Roman town had a public bathhouse, and sundials were used to regulate the separate opening times for men and women.

IDENTIFYING BUILDINGS

Archaeologists study Roman buildings and try to figure out their original design. Changes may have been made by non-Roman people who came along later and used a building for their own purposes. Even if a building is easy to identify, like a theater or a bathhouse, for example, it is not always easy to know when it was built. The basic design of many Roman buildings did not change a great deal over hundreds of years. Archaeologists have to look carefully for clues. A coin found on the site may have been dropped by someone a hundred years after it was built, but if the coin is found buried inside the building material, then it was probably dropped by one of the actual builders, and the date of the coin will reveal when the building was constructed.

MONUMENTS

Archaeologists benefit from the fact that the Romans loved to build monuments. If Rome was successful in a war, wealthy people often paid for a triumphal arch to be built in celebration. These arches were often built at the entrances to towns, and the men who paid for them could have their own inscriptions recorded on the stone. Historians of art are interested in the best examples of these inscriptions because of the artistic talent needed to cut letters into stone in an attractive way. Experts can often tell the rough age of a monument by examining the style of the lettering that makes up the inscription. Latin was the common language of the Roman world, but monuments from

The triumphal Arch of Severus, who was emperor between A.D. 193 and 211. Although the arch is here undergoing restoration, the inscriptions can still clearly be seen. Severus strengthened the imperial army and gained the Empire its final province, Mesopotamia, in A.D. 199. He died on campaign in northern Britain in A.D. 211.

eastern provinces often have inscriptions in Greek. Greek was the second most important language in the Roman Empire and was commonly used in the eastern Mediterranean area.

Memorial tombs were popular with wealthy families, and archaeologists have found a number of these. Like the triumphal arches, they were built of stone or marble. This has helped preserve them over the centuries. Inscriptions on tombs often describe the achievements of the dead person. It was also common to record the exact age of the person in years and months, and sometimes even days.

Monumental arches, gates, and tombs often had sculptures carved onto them. When a line of sculptures forms a band along one side of a monument, it is known as a frieze. A carefully cleaned frieze may show interesting information, especially if it is recording an actual event.

Only the wealthy could afford to be commemorated with a carved memorial tomb. This tomb shows "Augustus Hermia" and his wife.

Trajan's Column

The friezes that wind their way around Trajan's Column in Rome are of great interest to archaeologists and historians. There is no writing aside from an inscription at the base of the column, but the friezes form a kind of giant "picture book" that provides the most complete record we have of the Roman Army.

A frieze at the bottom of the column shows the Roman Army crossing the Danube River. The clothing and armor of the regular soldier, the legionary, are shown in great detail. Body armor, reaching from the shoulder to the hip, is worn over a tunic that comes halfway down the thigh. A shield hangs from one shoulder, while over the other hangs a helmet and a wooden stake that holds the legionary's gear.

Other friezes show the army in fighting action. We see first aid being given to the wounded, prisoners having their arms tied behind their backs, and examples of Roman machinery used in an attack. They used a spring-operated cannon that could fire from a cart, as well as battering rams and a mobile platform for reaching the tops of the walls of towns that were being attacked.

The base of Trajan's Column, showing Roman soldiers marching out of a walled town and crossing the Danube using boat-bridges. The figure with a crown of reeds is "Father Danube."

PROJECT: MAKE AN INSCRIPTION

You will need:
Cardboard
Scissors
Modeling clay
Rolling pin
Modeling tool

I = 1
V = 5
X = 10
L = 50
C = 100
D = 500
M = 1,000

Cut out a piece of cardboard about 6 in. (15 cm) long and 2 in. (5 cm) wide. Roll out the modeling clay so that it completely covers the cardboard on one side. Use the modeling tool to inscribe your birthday (e.g., 11.10.90) in Roman numerals.

Writing extra numerals after a numeral gives a higher number (e.g., VII = 7), and writing them before a numeral gives a lower number (e.g., IV = 4).

THE EMPEROR TRAJAN

Trajan was born in Spain in A.D. 52. Under his rule the Roman Empire reached its greatest size. He invaded and defeated a country that was then known as Dacia. Nowadays, the country is named after its Roman conquerors: Romania. After Trajan returned in triumph to Rome, public games and gladiator fights celebrated his success for months. Trajan's Column was put up in A.D. 113. It is made up of 17 huge rounded blocks of marble and is nearly 100 ft. (30 m) high. Pictures spiral around the column over 20 times. After Trajan's death his ashes were placed inside the base of the column. Historians consider Trajan to be one of Rome's greatest emperors.

Trajan died in A.D. 117, falling ill while returning to Rome after defending the Empire in the East. Hadrian claimed that Trajan had adopted him on his deathbed, and Hadrian became the next emperor.

PRESERVING THE PAST

Trajan's Column has stood in the center of Rome for nearly 2,000 years, but it does not follow that it will safely remain there for another 2,000 years. The pollution in a modern city like Rome is a threat to any building or monument that is

Conservation work is necessary today in order to protect Roman buildings for the future.

exposed to the air. Even if a site that is away from traffic and factories has been excavated, there is still the problem of weather. Gradually, over a long period of time, the wind, rain, and sun will damage what archaeologists have unearthed. Preserving the past for future generations, and not just for our own immediate benefit, is a challenge facing archaeologists.

If an archaeological site is very popular, the large number of visitors creates a serious problem. At the Roman town of Ephesus, many thousands of tourists trudge through the theater, library, houses, and other remains every year. Not everyone understands the need to treat places like Ephesus with care and respect. At Pompeii some tourists even add graffiti to the wall paintings. There is also a problem protecting large sites from thieves who try to steal the valuable artifacts.

Sometimes it is not possible to preserve an entire site. Parts of many large cities in Europe, including London, Paris, and Vienna, have been built over Roman settlements, and modern building work can accidentally uncover evidence of the past. A bulldozer may be clearing land for a new subway station and come across the important remains of a Roman building. When there is only a short amount of time for archaeologists to work on a site like this, their work is known as "rescue archaeology."

"Rescue archaeology": an archaeologist makes detailed notes on a site that will soon become the foundation for a modern building.

WHAT NEXT?

When Pompeii was first excavated in the nineteenth century, gunpowder was used to clear the site. Archaeology has come a long way since then, and archaeologists no longer take the remains of monuments away to enrich museums in their own countries. Instead, as we have seen, a variety of scientific methods are now used to investigate the past. However, when a site is being excavated and artifacts are examined, it is impossible to avoid some destruction.

Archaeologists of the future, looking back at what is being done today, may be shocked at what they see as our primitive methods. In the future there will be new scientific methods. This should lead to more information about the world of the Romans.

Today's archaeologists recognize this and try to make allowances. At large sites an area may be deliberately unexcavated and left alone for the future. If an artifact is found to be repairable, restoration work should not make any changes that cannot be undone at some later time. In this way, the past is being conserved for the sake of the future.

Modern archaeology makes use of a wide variety of tools and machines, all designed to make excavation more efficient. "Mini-diggers" like this are sometimes used on large sites during the early stages of excavation.

Methods are being developed to use computers to reconstruct archaeological sites in three dimensions. Computer-generated pictures of Roman buildings create a convincing sense of how they might once have looked. New forms of "virtual reality" will allow people to see pictures of a Roman ship or Trajan's Column as if they were looking at the real thing.

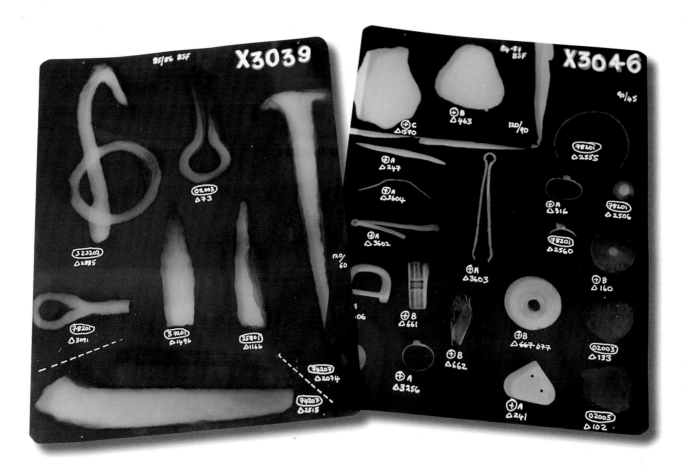

This does not mean the end of archaeology. People who are interested in the past will always enjoy seeing real physical artifacts and other remains. Archaeologists will continue to excavate sites, although their methods and equipment may be different. History is still beneath your feet.

X rays can reveal important information without changing or damaging the original artifact. This is one of the aims of archaeologists.

TIME LINES

ANCIENT ROMAN TIME LINE

900 B.C.	575 B.C.	509 B.C.	312 B.C.	260 B.C.
The first Romans living on hilltops (see page 4)	Forum built in Rome (see pages 4–5)	Creation of the Roman Republic (see page 4)	Appian Way built (see page 11)	The first navy of Roman ships is built (see page 12)

A.D. 43	A.D. 54	A.D. 79	A.D. 80	A.D. 113
Conquest of Britain under Claudius (see page 25)	Nero becomes emperor (see page 25)	Towns of Pompeii and Herculaneum buried beneath volcanic ash and mud (see pages 14, 17, 19, 41)	The Colosseum is opened in Rome (see page 19)	Trajan's Column is completed in Rome (see pages 38–39)

ARCHAEOLOGICAL TIME LINE (ALL DATES ARE A.D.)

1593	1763	1864	1875	1910	1954
A part of Pompeii discovered for the first time but the importance of the find was not then understood	Pompeii "rediscovered" and the importance of the site realized	Fiorelli begins work on plaster-cast figures at Pompeii (see page 29)	Mark Twain visits Roman sites on a Mediterranean cruise and writes about what he sees for the American public	A seagoing Roman merchant ship is accidentally discovered by workmen in the Thames River, London	The "Temple of Mithras" discovered in London. It is reconstructed 165 ft. (50 m) away from the original site to allow the construction of a modern building

44 B.C.	27 B.C.	20 B.C.
Julius Caesar, dictator of Rome since 47 B.C., assassinated	Augustus becomes the first emperor (see page 4)	Aqueduct built in France, crossing the Gard River (see pages 30–31)

A.D. 117	A.D. 330	A.D. 476
Trajan dies and Hadrian becomes emperor (see page 39)	Constantinople becomes the main city of the Roman Empire (see page 5)	End of the Roman Empire in the West (see page 5)

1977	1987	1990	1998
A Roman wreck discovered by a French Navy submersible in the Mediterranean at a depth of 1,076 ft. (328 m) (see page 13)	Parts of a Roman amphitheater discovered under a site called Guildhall Yard, in London	Valuable artifacts stolen by art thieves from Herculaneum	An Italian archaeologist uncovers a 2,000-year-old fresco while excavating near the Colosseum in Rome. The fresco shows an aerial view of an ancient city, possibly Rome itself

GLOSSARY

amphitheater roofless, oval-shaped building used for public shows.

amphora pottery vessel, usually with two handles, for holding and transporting wine or olive oil.

aqueduct an artificial channel for carrying water.

artifact an object made by humans, usually small enough to be carried by hand.

atrium central courtyard of a Roman house.

circus arena where chariot races were held.

citizenship all free-born citizens of Rome had the same full legal rights. Freedmen and freedwomen had fewer rights, and slaves had none at all.

corrosion the process of wearing away and decay by natural causes.

decompression sickness also known as the bends, this can affect divers who have spent too long beneath the water and return to the surface too quickly.

denarius an ancient Roman silver coin.

Etruria an area in north-west Italy where people developed a civilization before the rise of Rome.

excavate dig into the ground in an organized way in order to uncover archaeological remains.

forum center of social and political life in a Roman town.

hypocaust space for underfloor hot-air heating in ancient Roman houses and baths.

insulae large tenements or apartment buildings where the mass of the population in Rome lived. The small, single rooms were rented to lodgers, and the *insulae* soon gained a reputation for being overcrowded and unsafe.

mosaic thousands of small pieces of glass, stone, or other materials joined together to form a pattern and pressed into cement. Mosaics were used to decorate floors and walls.

peristyle the enclosed garden of a Roman house or villa, usually surrounded by colonnaded walkways.

province in ancient Rome, a territory outside Italy under the control of a Roman governor.

republic government by elected representatives.

shards broken pieces of pottery.

stylus sharp-pointed instrument used for writing on wax tablets.

FURTHER INFORMATION

BOOKS

Barghusen, Joan D. *Daily Life in Ancient and Modern Rome* (Cities Through Time). Minneapolis, MN: Lerner Publications, 1999.

Chrisp, Peter. *The Colosseum* (Great Buildings). Austin, TX: Raintree Steck-Vaughn, 1999.

Ganeri, Anita. *How Would You Survive as an Ancient Roman* (How Would You Survive). Danbury, CT: Franklin Watts, 1995.

James, Louise. *How We Know About the Romans* (How We Know About). New York: Peter Bedrick Books, 1997.

James, Simon. *Ancient Rome* (Eyewitness). New York: Knopf Books for Young Readers, 1990

Kerr, Daisy. *Ancient Romans* (Worldwise). Danbury, CT: Franklin Watts, 1997.

Sheehan, Sean and Pat Levy. *Rome* (Ancient World). Austin, TX: Raintree Steck-Vaughn, 1999.

Simpson, Judith. *Ancient Rome* (Nature Company Discoveries Library). Alexandria, VA: Time-Life Books, 1997.

Snedden, Robert. *Technology in the Time of Ancient Rome* ((Technology in the Time of). Austin, TX: Raintree Steck-Vaughn, 1999.

Steele, Philip. *Food and Feasts in Ancient Rome*. New York: New Discovery, 1995.

WEBSITES

The Ancient World Wide Web site has a good section on ancient Rome: http://www.julen.net/aw/

Pictures of ancient Roman sites, portraits of the emperors and a chat line can all be found at: http://ancienthistory.miningco.com/msubjulio.htm

Good educational material on ancient Rome along with useful links to other sites is available at: http://members.aol.com/Donnclass/Romelife.html

INDEX

Numbers in **bold** refer to illustrations